Jumbo Jets

Blaine Wiseman

WEIGL PUBLISHERS INC.
"Creating Inspired Learning"
www.weigl.com

Published by Weigl Publishers Inc.
350 5th Avenue, 59th Floor
New York, NY 10118
Website: www.weigl.com

Library of Congress Cataloging-in-Publication Data

Wiseman, Blaine.
 Jumbo jets / Blaine Wiseman.
    p. cm. -- (Wow big machines)
 Includes bibliographical references and index.
 ISBN 978-1-61690-136-3 (hardcover : alk. paper) -- ISBN 978-1-61690-137-0 (softcover : alk. paper) -- ISBN 978-1-61690-138-7 (e-book)
 1. Jet transports--Juvenile literature. I. Title.
 TL547.W724 2011
 629.133'349--dc22

                                    2010013936

Printed in the United States of America in North Mankato, Minnesota
2 3 4 5 6 7 8 9 0 15 14 13 12 11

022011
WEP040211

Editor: Heather C. Hudak
Design: Terry Paulhus

Weigl acknowledges Getty Images as its primary image supplier for this title.

CONTENTS

What are Jumbo Jets?

Have you ever seen a huge metal object racing through the sky? This may have been an airplane. The biggest airplanes are called jumbo jets. One jumbo jet can carry hundreds of people at one time. These jets also carry huge loads of goods from one place to another.

The U.S. president has his own jumbo jet. It carries him, his family, and his staff around the world. This special plane is known as Air Force One.

Supersize

How big are jumbo jets? Jumbo jets come in many sizes. The first jumbo jet was the Boeing 747. It could carry as many as 490 people at once.

Today, the world's biggest jumbo jet is the Airbus A380. This massive machine can carry more than 800 people on one flight.

A fully loaded Airbus A380 can weigh more than 1 million pounds (453,592 kilograms). This is about as much as three blue whales.

Jumbo Materials

Did you know that some jumbo jets are made from the same type of metal as soda cans? This lightweight metal is used to make the body, or fuselage, of some jumbo jets.

Some materials, such as plastic, are longer lasting than lightweight metal. Parts made from these materials need to be replaced less often. They do not wear down over time from rust or overuse.

Big and Fast

Have you ever seen a jumbo jet take off? Jumbo jets must reach incredible speeds to fly. A fully loaded Boeing 747 will reach speeds of about 180 miles (290 kilometers) per hour before takeoff.

In the air, a jumbo jet can travel more than 600 miles (966 km) per hour. This is about 10 times faster than the speed of cars driving on a highway.

Flying High

How do jumbo jets lift off the ground? There are special **forces** that help jumbo jets fly. The jet's powerful engines create a force that moves the jet forward. The wings of an airplane create a force that raises the jet into the air. High speeds help jets create the forces they need to fly.

Jumbo jets carrying people often fly 30,000 to 40,000 feet (9,144 to 12,192 meters) above the ground. This is as high as 30 to 40 Empire State Buildings stacked on top of each other.

Long Range

How far do jumbo jets fly? Jumbo jets fly all over the world. The Boeing 777-200LR Worldliner can carry 300 passengers 10,800 miles (17,381 km) without landing.

Flying at slower speeds uses less fuel. Some flights last less than one hour. Others can take much longer. The longest passenger flight in the world is from Newark, New Jersey, to Singapore. This flight lasts almost 19 hours.

Landing Gear

How does a jumbo jet take off and land without sliding on its belly? Jumbo jets use special sets of wheels, tires, brakes, **struts**, and other parts for takeoff and landing. These parts are known as landing gear.

Landing gear is pulled back into the jet after takeoff. The gear comes down again at the end of the flight. It supports the jet as it touches the ground.

A Boeing 747 has seven sets of landing gear. There are two sets under each wing, two under the body, and one under the nose.

The Flight Deck

Where does the pilot sit to drive a jumbo jet? The pilot sits in a room called the flight deck, or cockpit. The flight deck is at the front of the jet. It is filled with buttons, knobs, and **levers** that control the jet. From here, the pilot can see where the jet is flying, speak over the radio, and adjust the jet's speed.

Pilots spend years training in smaller planes before they can fly a jumbo jet.

19

Keeping Clean

Did you know that jumbo jets made from lightweight materials use less fuel? Using less fuel helps the environment. This is because fewer **pollutants** are released into the air. Scientists also are trying to find cleaner fuels for jumbo jets.

Taking Flight

scissors   paper

1. With an adult's help, cut the piece of paper in half, lengthwise.

2. Hold one end of the paper firmly between your thumb and index finger.

3. With the paper facing away from you, blow over the top of the paper.

4. What happens to the paper? Imagine that the paper is the wing of a jumbo jet, and think about how wind helps lift a jet off the ground.

Find Out More

To learn more about jumbo jets, visit these websites.

Science Kids at Home
www.sciencekidsathome.com/science_topics/flight.html

ALLSTAR Network
www.allstar.fiu.edu/aero/fltmidcont.htm

Crayola
www.crayola.com/crafts/
detail/build-a-jumbo-jet-craft/

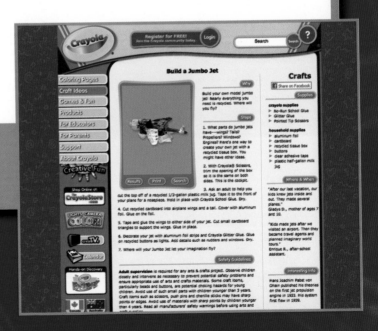

Glossary

forces: powerful effects that produce a change

levers: bars or rods that control parts of a machine

pollutants: waste materials that harm the air, soil, or water

struts: bars or rods that keep a vehicle stable

Index